Bill Evans
alone

Transcribed by Aaron Prado

Bill Evans Estate is Administered by Nenette Evans
30441 Via Elcazar
Laguna Niguel, CA 92677-2137

ISBN: 978-1-4950-2252-4

CORPORATION

7777 W. BLUEMOUND RD. P.O. BOX 13819 MILWAUKEE, WI 53213

Visit Hal Leonard Online at
www.halleonard.com

TRANSCRIPTION NOTES

Bill Evans's album *Alone* is a landmark of solo piano in modern jazz. Recorded in the fall of 1968 and released in 1970, it represents a turning point away from the prominent solo piano styles of the past, including Stride, Swing, and early Bebop towards a modern approach to unaccompanied playing. While subsequent CD issues included numerous "alternate" takes and some different repertoire, the transcriptions contained in this folio include only the five master takes issued on the original LP release.

For best results, these transcriptions should be used in conjunction with the recordings to bring out the nuances of phrasing, dynamics, and feeling Evans achieved in creating these masterful performances. There are many subtle shifts in tempo and rhythmic feeling – and this lines up with Evans's stated approach to solo playing, as described during an interview with *Downbeat* magazine in 1976:

 "My conception of solo playing is a music that moves; let's say a more rhapsodic conception that has interludes of straight-ahead jazz. It would be a more orchestral conception, moving very freely between keys and moods. In other words, things you can't do with a group. That's the added dimension."

Of all the performances, "Never Let Me Go" is by far the longest and features the richest array of melodic and harmonic variation. A few notes about this transcription:

- Intricate chromatic embellishment is a basic feature of the performance; each distinct chromatic change in the harmony is acknowledged in the chord symbols only in the first chorus, then the chord symbols are somewhat simplified to primarily reflect basic root motion thereafter.
- The piece is taken at a very slow and steady pace but gradually the tempo climbs from about 55 BPM to around 70 BPM during the improvisation – again, let the recording be your guide regarding tempo fluctuation.
- Also use the recording to determine when double-time passages include "swung" sixteenth notes and thirty-second notes versus "straight" rhythmic passages found in melody statements.
- Finally, note the extensive use of distinct "voices" in the left hand, a key feature of Evans's sound and style. For maximum clarity, limit use of the sustain pedal to bring out the sophisticated balance of note durations in the left hand voices.

Dr. Aaron Prado - 2015

CONTENTS

Here's That Rainy Day

As performed by Bill Evans on "Alone"- Verve 9428

Words by Johnny Burke
Music by Jimmy Van Heusen

Freely, flowing

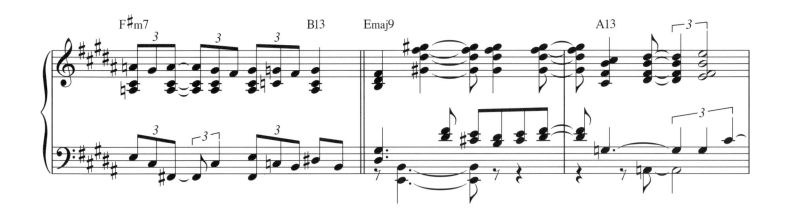

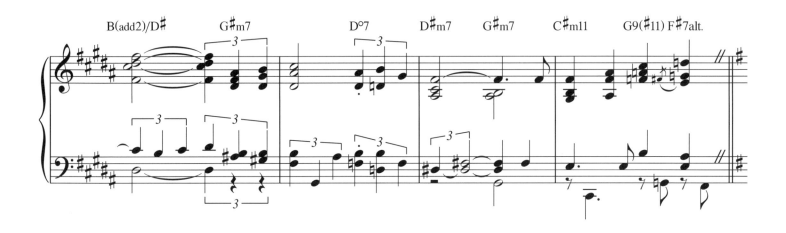

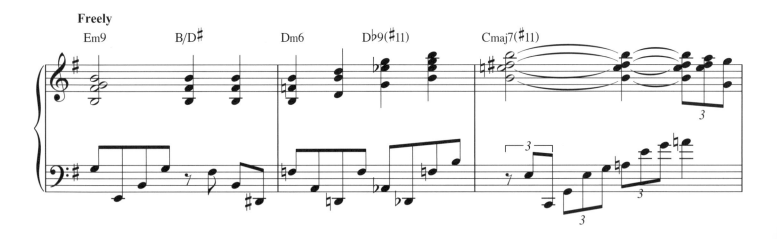

A Time for Love

As performed by Bill Evans on "Alone" - Verve 9428

Music by Johnny Mandel
Words by Paul Francis Webster

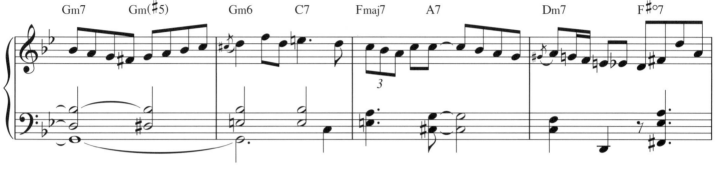

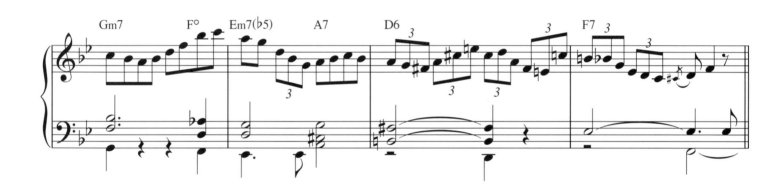

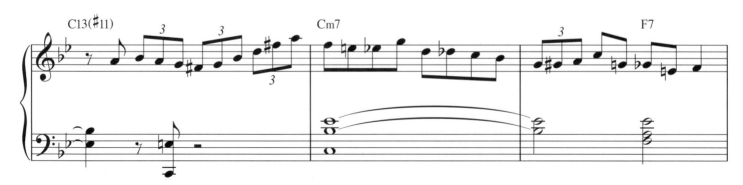

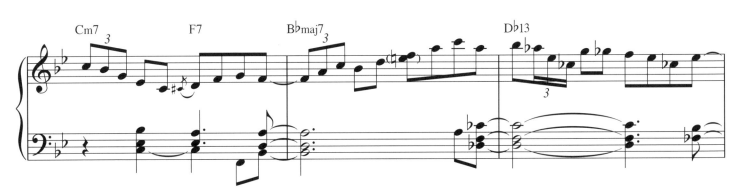

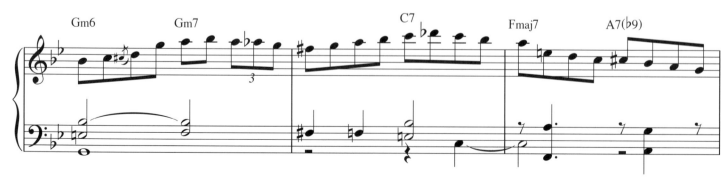

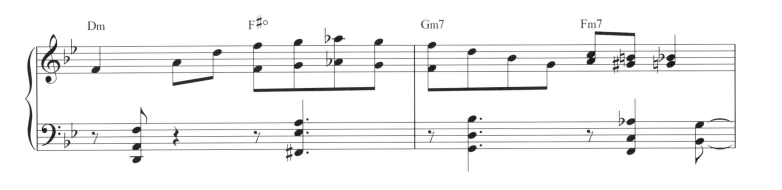

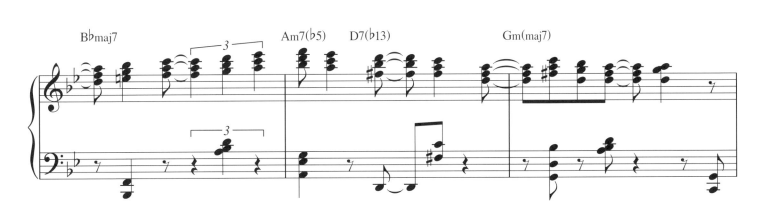

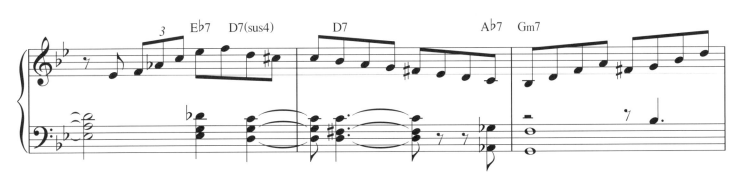

Midnight Mood

As performed by Bill Evans on "Alone" - Verve 9428
By Joe Zawinul

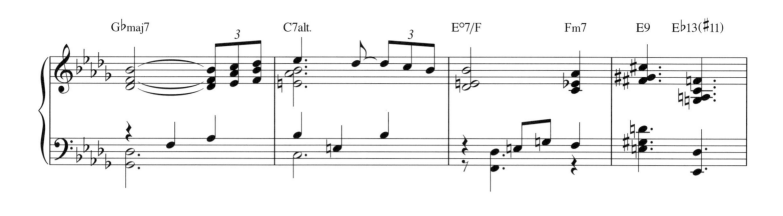

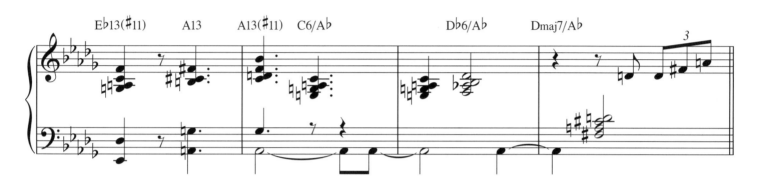

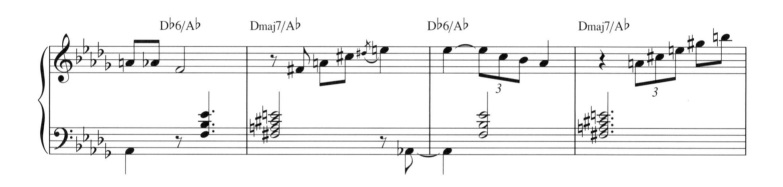

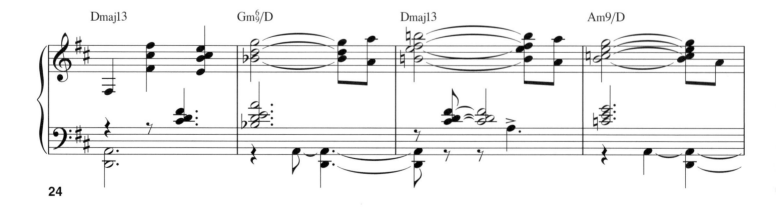

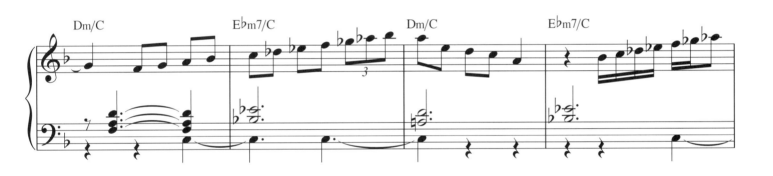

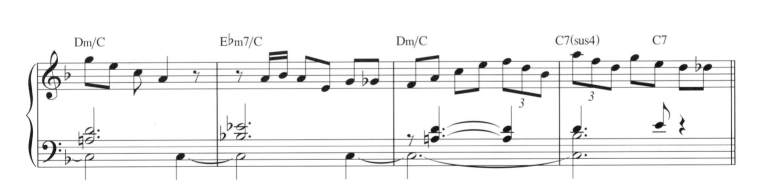

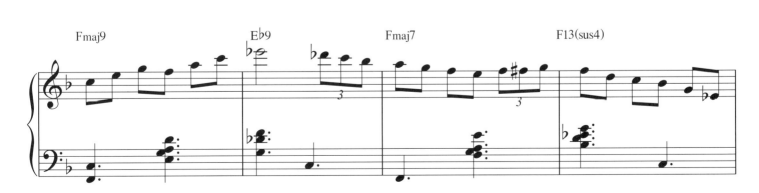

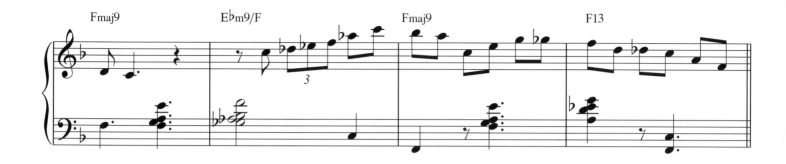

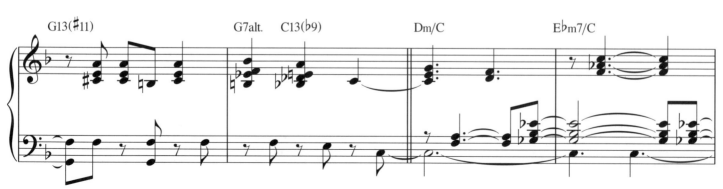

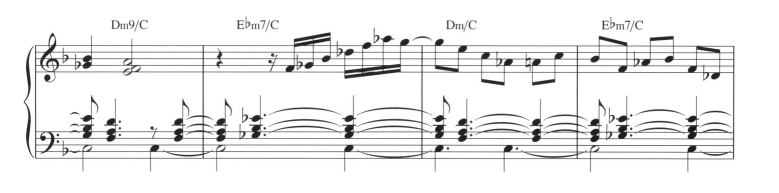
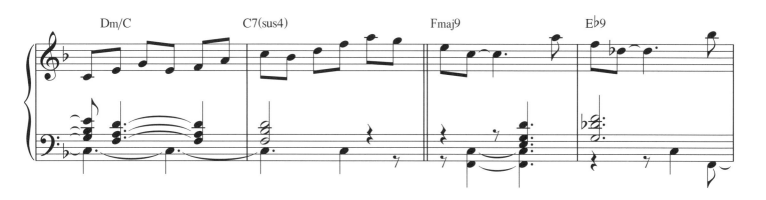
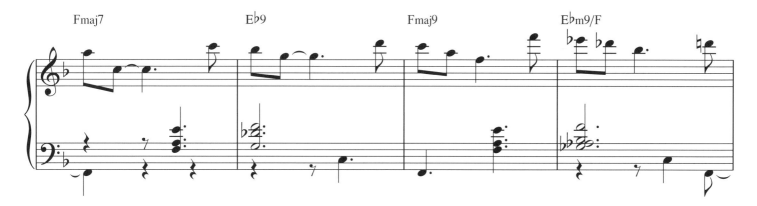
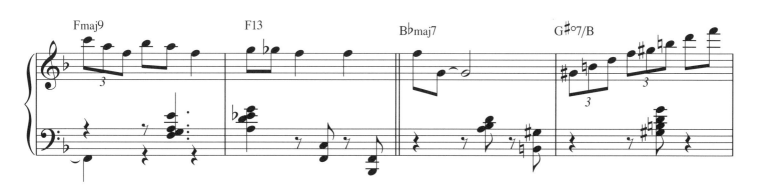

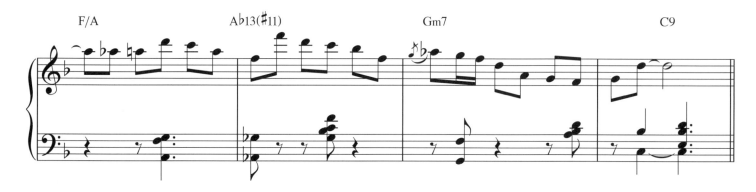

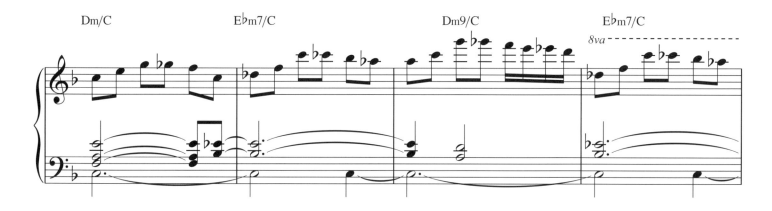

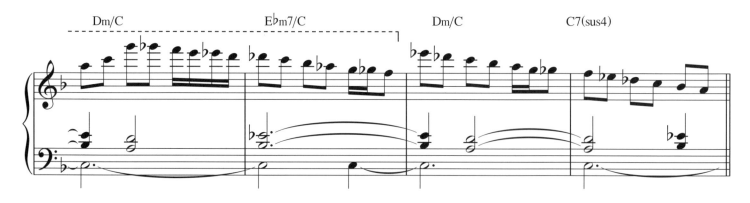

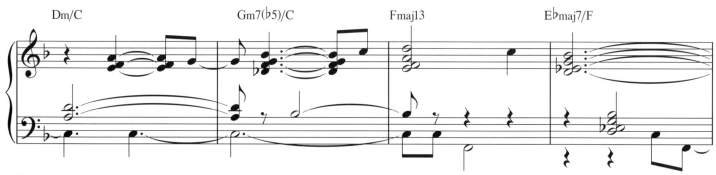

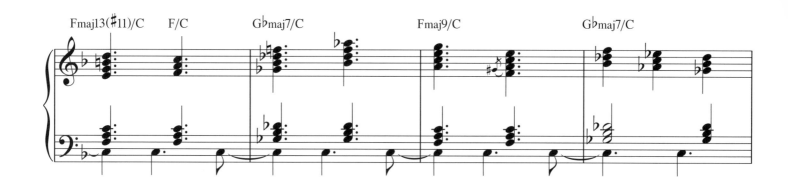

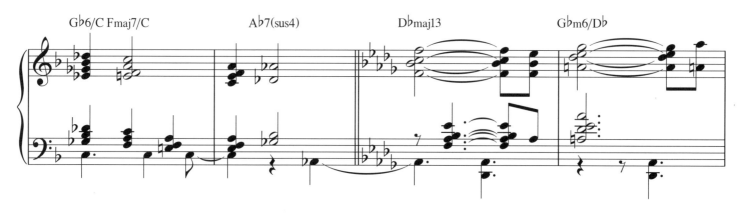

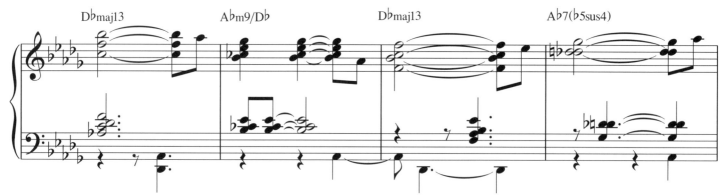

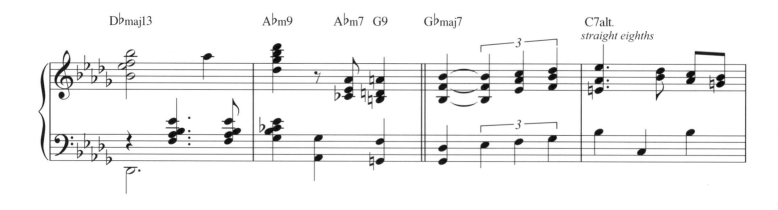

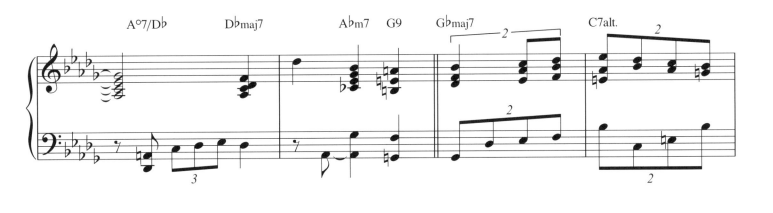

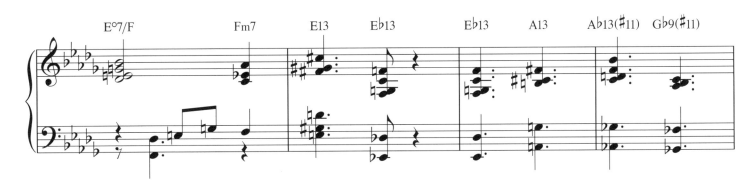

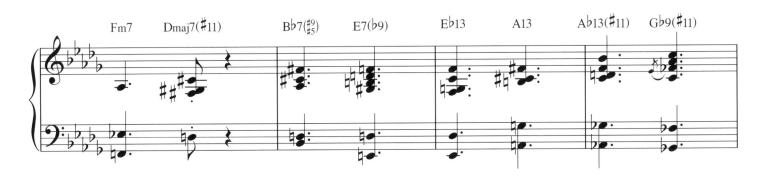

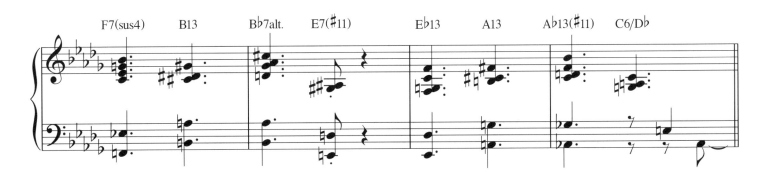

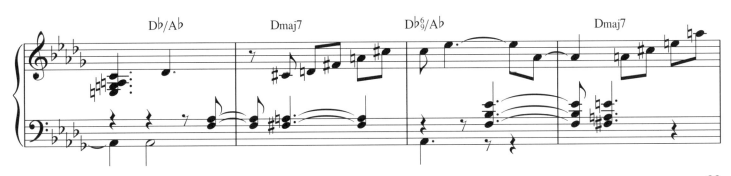

On a Clear Day

(You Can See Forever)

from ON A CLEAR DAY YOU CAN SEE FOREVER

As performed by Bill Evans on "Alone"- Verve 9428

Words by Alan Jay Lerner
Music by Burton Lane

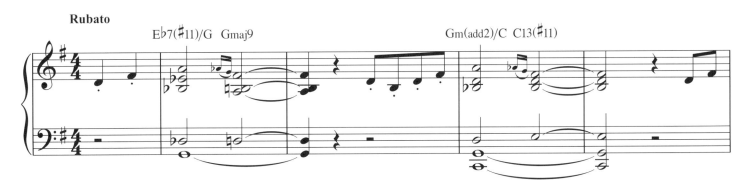

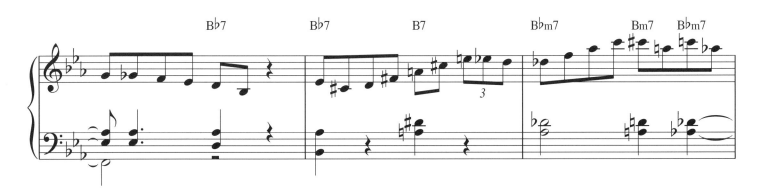

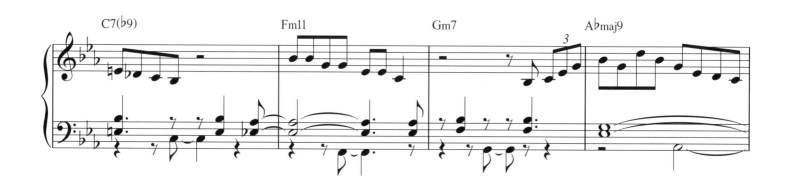

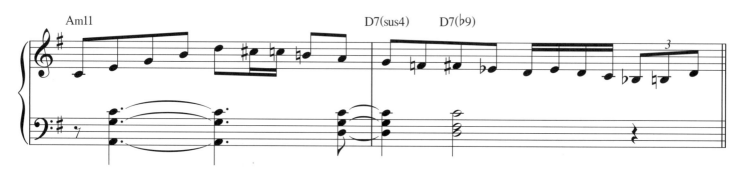

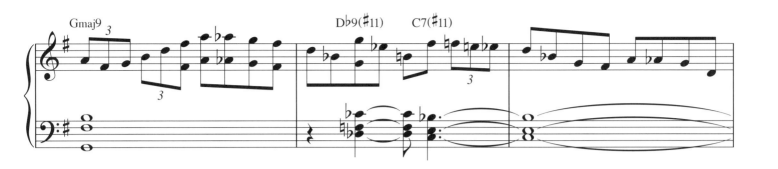

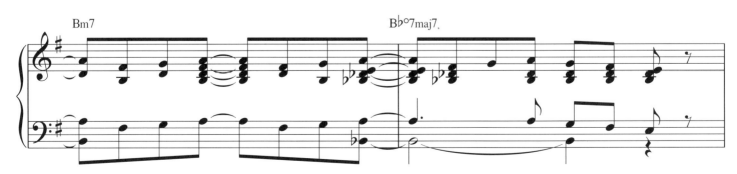

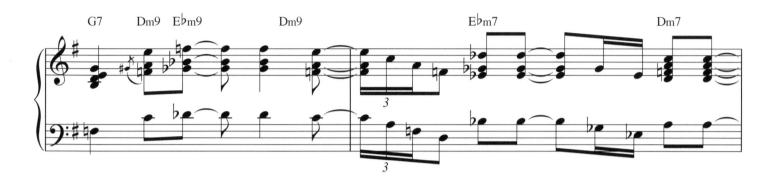

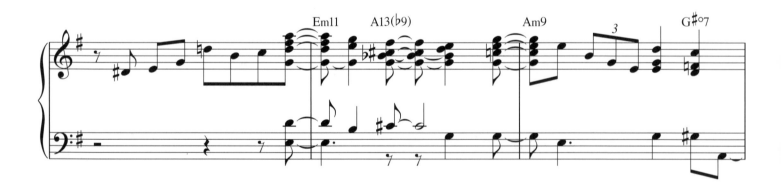

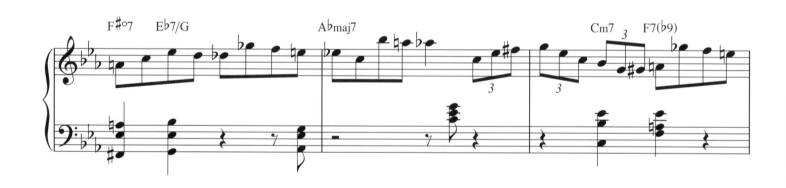

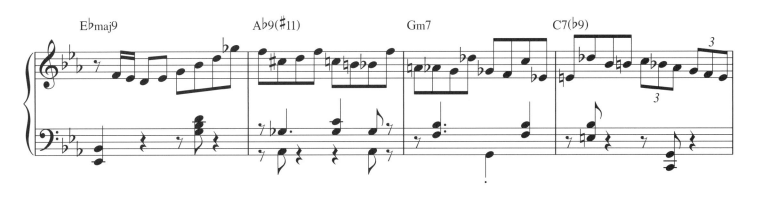

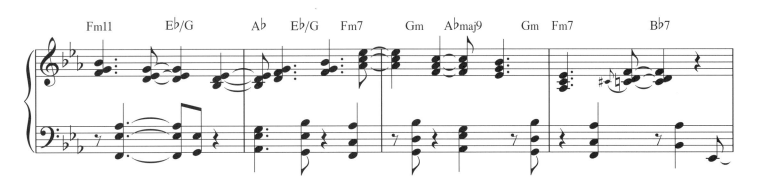

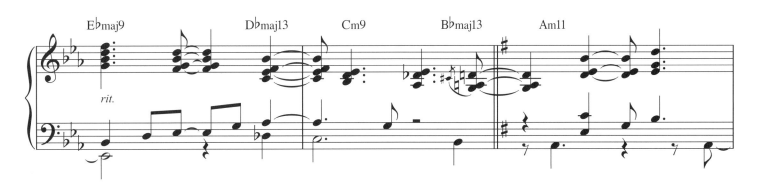

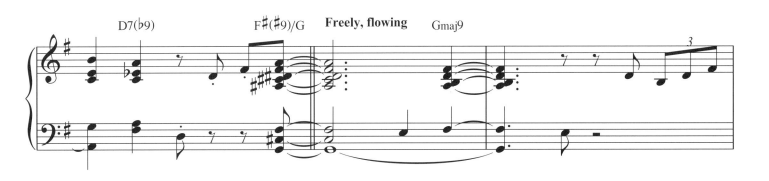

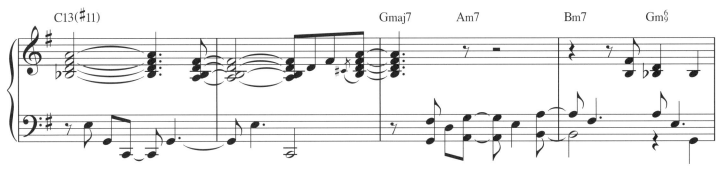

Never Let Me Go

from the Paramount Picture THE SCARLET HOUR
As performed by Bill Evans on "Alone"- Verve 9428
Words and Music by Jay Livingston and Ray Evans

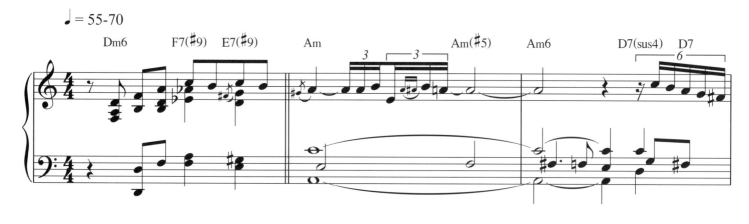

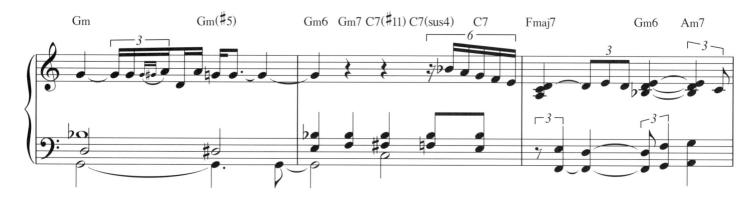

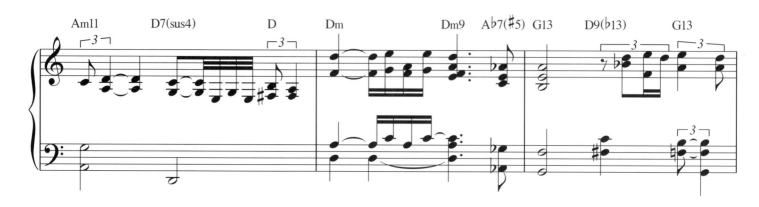

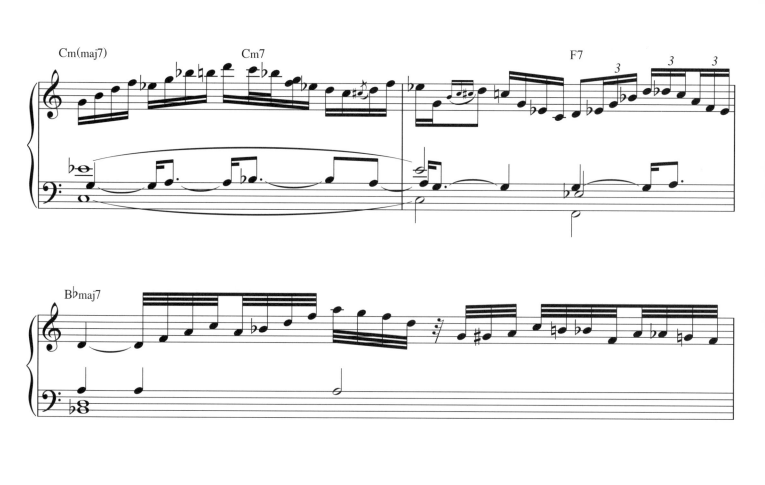

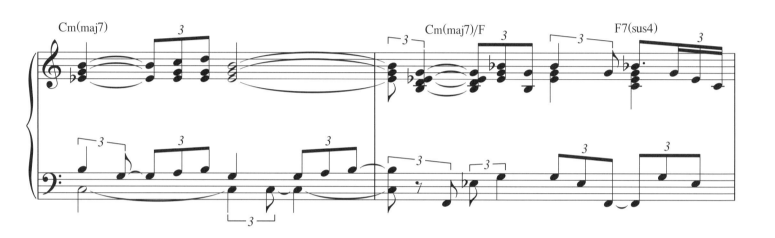

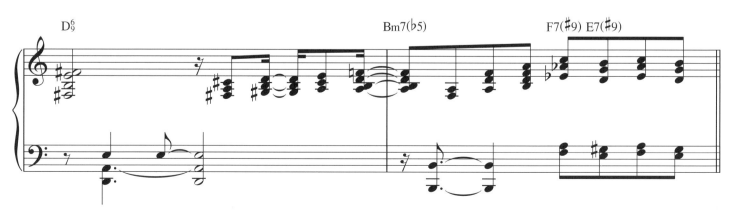

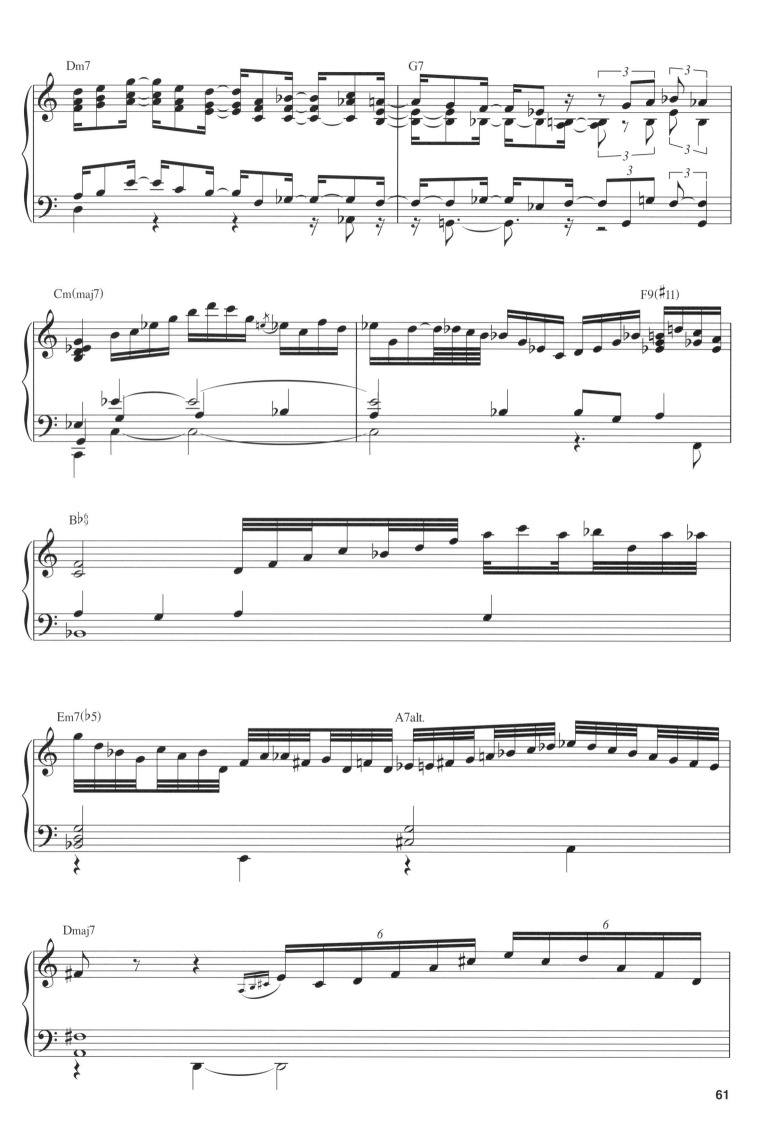

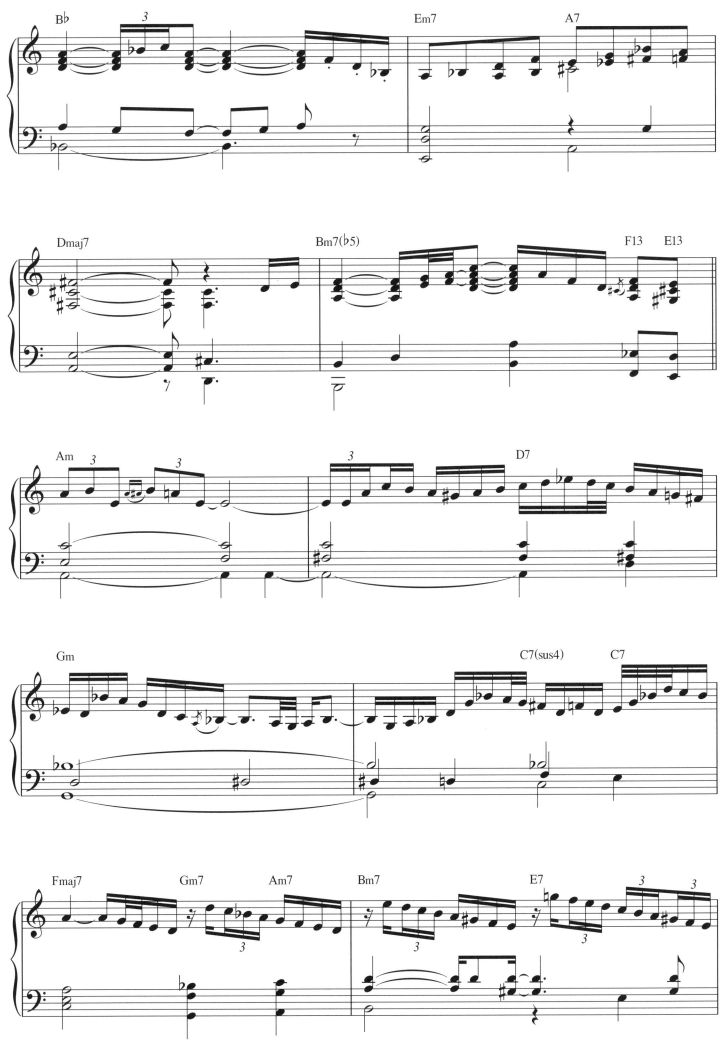

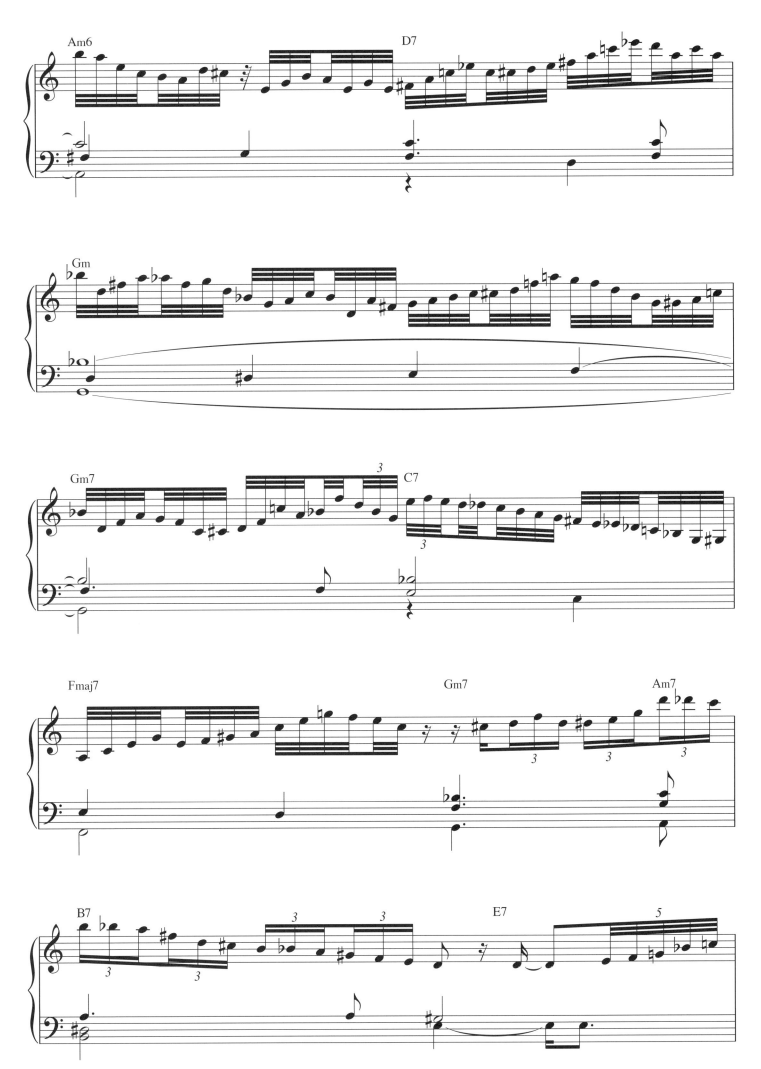

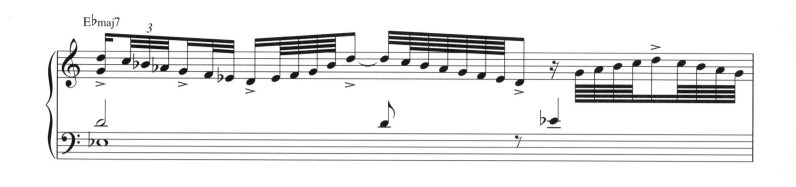

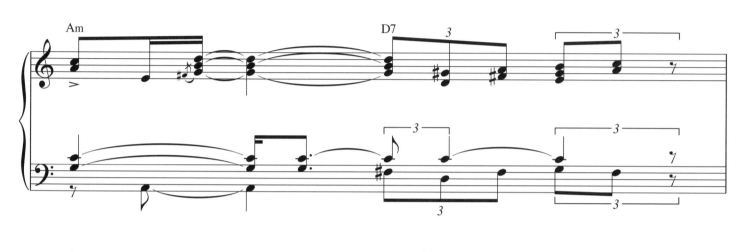

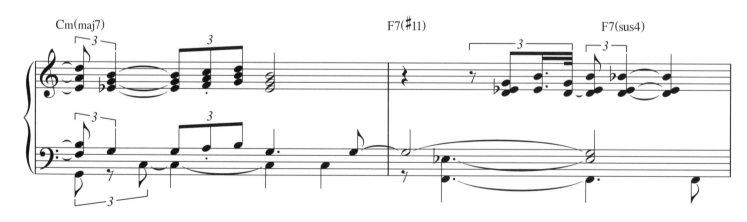

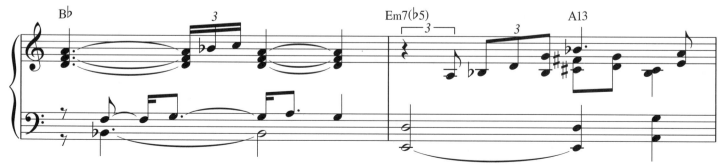

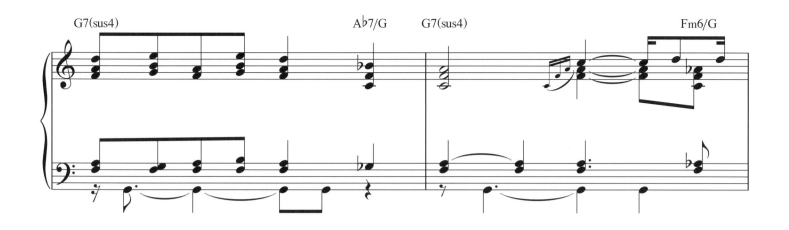

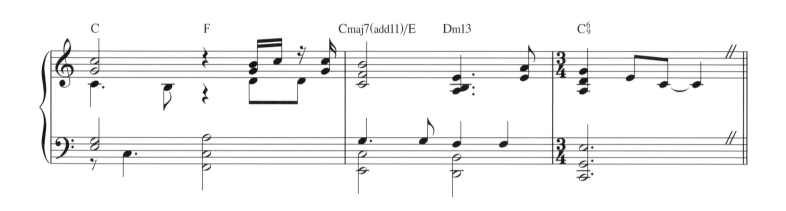

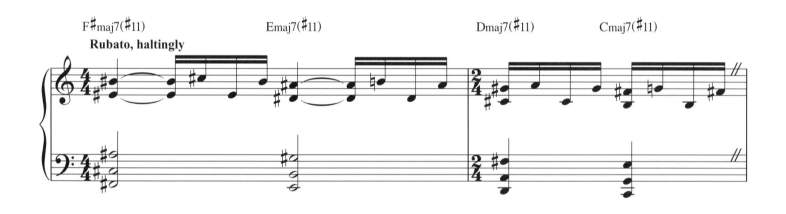